FINANCIAL HAPPINESS
IN TWO HOURS
A YEAR

FINANCIAL HAPPINESS IN TWO HOURS A YEAR

Ways To Enjoy Life More And Worry Less

CHRIS HASENBERG

Copyright © 2024 by Chris Hasenberg

All rights reserved. No part of this publication may be reproduced, distributed or transmitted in any form or by any means, including photocopying, recording, or other electronic or mechanical methods, without the prior written permission of the publisher, except in the case of brief quotations embodied in critical reviews and certain other noncommercial uses permitted by copyright law. For permission requests, write to the publisher, addressed "Attention: Permissions Coordinator," at the email address below.

Chris Hasenberg
info@hasenberginc.com
www.hasenberginc.com

Financial Happiness In Two Hours A Year, Chris Hasenberg —1st ed.

DISCLAIMER

*Securities offered through Purshe Kaplan Sterling Investments, Member FINRA/SIPC Headquartered at 80 State Street, Albany, NY 12207. Purshe Kaplan Sterling Investments and Hasenberg Financial Group are not affiliated companies.

The information presented is believed to be factual and up to date, but we do not guarantee its accuracy and it should not be regarded as a complete analysis of the subjects discussed. Discussions and answers to questions do not involve the rendering of personalized investment advice but are limited to the dissemination of general information. A professional advisor should be consulted before implementing any of the options presented.

Hasenberg Financial Group is registered as an investment advisor with the SEC and only transacts business in states where it is properly registered or is excluded or exempted from registration requirements.

DISCLOSURE

Important Note on Legal Advice

This book is intended to provide general information about financial planning topics, including estate planning. While efforts have been made to ensure the accuracy of the information presented, it is not intended to be legal advice. Laws and regulations regarding financial and estate planning vary by jurisdiction and may change over time.

Readers are advised that the information contained in this book should not be relied upon as a substitute for personalized legal advice from a qualified attorney or other professional familiar with your individual situation. Estate planning involves complex considerations that may require specific legal knowledge and expertise.

Before making any decisions or taking any actions based on the information in this book, it is recommended that you consult with a licensed attorney or legal advisor who can provide guidance tailored to your particular circumstances and applicable laws.

CONTENTS

Introduction *11*

1. A Shift in Purpose 15
2. What Will Your Legacy Be? 23
3. What You Have and Where You Have It 39
4. Know Your Number..47
5. 12 Steps to Financial Independence..................................53
6. What is an Estate Plan (and Why Do You Need It)?............63
7. Planning for Incapacity 69
8. What Happens If You Die Without an Estate Plan? 73
9. Wills and Trusts...79
10. Taxes 87
11. Long-Term Care and Nursing Homes 105
12. Your Financial Team 111
13. Hindsight is 20/20 121

About the Author..*125*

The author and publisher disclaim any liability, loss, or risk incurred as a consequence, directly or indirectly, of the use and application of any of the contents of this book.

INTRODUCTION

Why did you open this book?

Odds are, you're not reading a book about financial happiness just for fun…

Most likely, you have something weighing on your mind. Maybe you're approaching retirement age and wondering if you've saved enough. Perhaps a recent health scare made you realize that you don't have an estate plan. You might be troubled by media stories about inflation, taxes, or Social Security.

No matter what your story is, your problem boils down to this: *fear of the unknown.*

Imagine setting off on a road trip with no map or GPS to guide you. The road is foggy, and you have no idea what lies ahead. Sounds terrifying, doesn't it?

Before you've created plans for your retirement and estate, that's how this chapter of your life can feel—terrifying. How can you wrap your mind around issues like Social Security, taxes, wills, inflation, and everything else you know you're supposed to consider?. That sense of fear only grows when you hear all the noise in the media about poor Social Security outlooks, rising taxes, and the struggles of putting enough away for retirement in this economy.

Just as you need a map to navigate unknown terrain and reach your destination, you need a financial plan that charts a clear path to your goals.

The road to finanical happiness is easier with a guide.

My goal in this book is to be that guide, equipping you with the information you need to begin your financial happiness journey.

The way to eliminate fear of the unknown is to become knowledgeable and, by the time you finish this book, you'll know the most important facts about:

- How much you need to retire
- Estate planning
- Planning for incapacity
- Avoiding probate

- Wills and trusts
- Taxes
- Planning for nursing homes or long-term care
- Building your financial team
- Leaving a financial legacy you're proud of

And so much more.

Armed with this information, you can do this on your own or you'll have the confidence you need to seek out a trusted financial advisor and begin creating a financial strategy that helps you accomplish your unique goals, like:

- Retiring when you want (and with the lifestyle you want)
- Ensuring you don't leave a "mess" for your loved ones when you pass away
- Having your estate distributed according to your desires, not the court's desires
- Minimizing the amount of your estate that is lost to taxes
- Preparing for unexpected health expenses (i.e. medications, nursing homes, etc.)

Above all, once your plan is in place, you'll be able to **enjoy life more and worry less.**

Ever heard the saying, "The best time to plant a tree was twenty years ago. The second best time is now."?

When it comes to financial planning, the best time to start was years ago. The second best time is now. The earlier you begin, the easier it will be to capture opportunities and avoid potential dangers.

The road to your financial future lies ahead…

Let's build a roadmap to get you there.

CHAPTER 1

A Shift in Purpose

Do you know your "number"?

My uncle worked for thirty years in computer networking and security. After that time, the company offered him severance if he retired. He knew his "number"—the amount he needed to retire—and this severance, combined with his other savings and investments, would put him at that number. Burnt out and excited to retire, he accepted the offer.

However, despite reaching his goal, fear kept him up at night.

My uncle knew he hit the number he needed to save for retirement. But now that he was staring retirement in the face, he wondered if that number would be enough. What if he ran out of money? What if some unforeseen expenses forced him to lower his standard of living? What would he do once the paychecks were no longer coming every two weeks?

He also wondered how changes to his income would impact the cost of health insurance. His younger wife was still working and if she was to join him in retirement, he may have to rely on the Affordable Care Act for health insurance until she turned 65. "Will my insurance costs skyrocket if I retire? Will I still have enough to retire if I have to pay more for insurance each year?" he wondered.

My uncle isn't alone…

You likely have a number in your head as a goalpost for retirement. Yet when you finally reach it after years of hard work, you may begin to question whether it's enough.

All of the "what-ifs" swirl around your mind and fill you with fear and stress at a time when you should be celebrating the start of a new chapter.

Here are just a few of the questions you may be asking yourself:

"What if my change in income impacts my healthcare cost?"

"Will I have enough to take that trip I've always dreamed of?"

"What if there are unforeseen expenses that I haven't thought about?"

"What if the market crashes?"

"Will there be any money left to leave my kids and grandkids?"

"What if my spouse passes away prematurely?"

"What if my spouse or I end up in a nursing home?"

These questions fill you with dread and terror because you can't answer them. The key to letting go of that fear and beginning your retirement with confidence and peace of mind is knowing the answers to these questions.

How do we do that? We make a plan.

Planning a Road Trip

If you're going on a road trip, you don't just hop in your car and start driving. You make a plan.

What's the weather? Where will you stop for gas? What route will you take? Will you need to stay overnight at a hotel? What happens if you get a flat tire? Do you know an alternate route in case there's a traffic jam?

You consider all the "what-ifs" before you get in the car and start driving—and you should do the same for retirement.

Just as one traffic jam or flat tire can derail a road trip, all it takes is one illness, one broken hip, a market crash, an IRS audit, or an unexpected stay in a nursing home to throw off your retirement plan. But if you've considered these "what-ifs" ahead of time and made plans for how you'll deal with them, you'll still reach your destination.—even if you encounter obstacles

On a road trip, your GPS constantly adjusts and readjusts your route and arrival time. For example, if I'm driving to Madison, Wisconsin, which is about two and a half hours away, my GPS will provide an initial route and arrival time. If I stop for lunch, then when I return to the car, my GPS will show a new arrival time. It may even reroute me to avoid a traffic jam that occurred while I was enjoying my lunch. My travel plan is not set in stone. My destination is the same, but the way I get there and the time I arrive constantly shift as circumstances change.

It's the same when planning for retirement. Your plan is not a one-and-done document that remains frozen in time. Instead, think of it like a GPS that is constantly readjusting to ensure you reach your destination—even if you encounter obstacles.

Do you spend more time planning your next vacation than your retirement?

Think about the last trip you took. How much time did you spend packing, planning your travel route, coordinating with family members, and scheduling activities?

A trip is finite. It usually lasts no more than a few weeks. But your retirement could last for three or more decades...

What would happen if you dedicated just 2 hours a year to talking about retirement? Could you make that commitment?

You don't have to go on this journey alone. Just as you hire a travel agent to help you plan a trip, a financial advisor can help you plan the trip of your lifetime—retirement. Throughout this journey, your financial advisor acts as a coach, guiding you and helping you change your route as your journey unfolds.

A Shift in Purpose

My dad was an over-the-road truck driver, and when he retired, we threw him a retirement party, complete with a gathering and a cake. For him, retirement was a great event because he didn't have to get in that truck and drive down the road. He did that job for a paycheck, not because he liked it, so retirement was something to celebrate.

On the other hand, I absolutely love what I do and get more satisfaction from helping people than I do from cashing my paycheck. So, to me, retirement feels like a dirty word. I want to do this until I'm either mentally incompetent or too tired to help anymore.

What about you? How do you view retirement? Is it a glorious event you're looking forward to? Or are you nervous because you love what you do? It is important to understand the difference when you and your advisor develop your plan.

As you approach retirement, it's also important to consider not only your finances but also how your life will change. I believe that the number one condition of a happy retirement has more to do with your social connections than your bank balance.

Think about this: aside from your spouse, who are the five people you spend the most time with?

When I ask my clients this question, invariably, three or four of the five people are coworkers.

When you retire, not only are you losing the day-to-day purpose that your career gave you, but you may also be losing some of the people you spend the most time with. If you go bowling or attend trivia night with your coworkers after work, will you still get those invites when you don't see those people every weekday? If your buddy who sat at the desk across from you is still working, who will you call when you want to play golf or go out to lunch on a Tuesday afternoon? Is your spouse still working? How will that affect your days?

Many retirees are surprised to discover how much free time they suddenly have. When you're used to having your schedule filled with work, how will you fill this newfound free time? What will your new purpose be? You can only hunt, fish, and golf so much before you find yourself calling the local car dealership to ask about becoming a courtesy driver—just to get out of the house.

I like to joke with my clients that we know their retirement is successful if I call them and they don't know what day of the week it is. I asked my dad if he knew what day of the week it was and he giggled and said that if the big newspaper comes, that's church day. Of course, he was only kidding, but still, many people aren't prepared for the transition to a 24/7 weekend.

So what are you going to do when you no longer go to work?

In this book, we'll certainly cover the numbers, but it's equally important to reflect on how you're going to spend your retirement and who you're going to spend it with.

Remember, you wouldn't get in the car and start driving without a destination…

So what is your retirement destination? What do you want the next chapter of your life to look like? What will your new purpose be?

Take a moment to reflect. Once you know where you're headed, we can build the map.

CHAPTER 2

What Will Your Legacy Be?

Since we strive to have lifetime relationships with our clients and most of our clients are older than us, we find that, statistically, about one client passes away each month and we end up going to a lot of funerals and wakes.

There are two types of wakes—though they may look similar on the surface. The casket is at the front of the room, surrounded by flowers. The immediate family stands next to it, greeting visitors who have come to pay their respects. Friends, extended family, and neighbors stand in line waiting to speak to the immediate family, sharing well-wishes and fond memories of the deceased. While mourners wait in line, a PowerPoint of photos often plays. Every once in a while a funny photo appears and everyone in the room giggles as they remember the humor and spirit of the departed.

However, it's when I reach the front of the line and greet the son and daughter of the deceased, that it becomes clear which of the two types of wakes I'm attending.

At the first type, the son and daughter look at me with eyes full of despair and say, "I can't believe the mess Dad left us with."

At the second, the son and daughter say, "I'm so glad Dad took the time to spare us a mess and introduced us to someone who could help us through this process."

Which type of wake do you want for your family? Will you leave them with a mess, or will they be grateful that you took care of everything?

Common Misconceptions About Estate Planning

The biggest misconception about estate planning is: "I have a will… That's enough, right?"

A will is a set of written directions telling the probate court what to do with your stuff. If you only have a will, your estate will most likely go through probate. Later in the book, we'll explore in detail why this is something you want to avoid.

Recently, I decided to do some research. I went to the County Courthouse and found out how many people went through probate last year. Then, I called the State Capitol to find out how many people died in my county last year. I did the math and found out that over one-third of everyone who passed away in my county last year ended up going through probate in some way, shape, or form.

My goal is to make sure none of our clients go through probate.

So why do so many people end up going through probate? Usually, it's either because they didn't want to spend the money to hire a professional to help create their estate plan or they thought a will was enough.

There are times to be thrifty and save money, and there are times it's worth paying a professional. I understand the desire to save money, but sometimes, by not paying for important services, you're doing yourself more harm than good.

For example, I could cut my own hair, but I pay a barber to cut my hair because she works with hair every day and can see things I can't see. It's worth the money to have my haircut done right so I don't risk looking foolish because I decided to save a few bucks and do it myself.

When it comes to estate planning, it's worth the investment to hire an expert. When you're creating a financial durable power of attorney and potentially giving somebody else the power to handle your finances, that is not the time to try to save money by doing it yourself or skipping it altogether. This would be like spending $50,000 on a college education but refusing to spend $100 to have someone professionally prepare your resume.

In regards to estate planning, everyone's situation is different. For instance, if you only have one heir, your estate plan will be simpler than someone who has six heirs. Usually, when people have multiple heirs, they don't want to divide the estate equally. If you have six kids, there's a chance that one of them has taken a path in life that you don't approve of.

If this is the case, you may want to put your assets into a trust—if the wayward child cleans up their act and you decide to include them as an heir, it's easier to change one trust document than to change beneficiaries on every policy, retirement account, and bank account that you have. This situation is just one example of the ways that estate planning needs to be personalized to fit each family's unique needs. It is by no means a cookie-cutter process.

A common danger in estate planning is procrastination. So many people think, "I'll get around to it someday…"

In our office, we combat procrastination with a fun bet. Once we decide that it's the right time for a client to put together an estate plan, we'll give the client a six-month time frame to get it done. If the client completes the estate plan in time, we'll buy them dinner. If they don't complete it, they have to buy us dinner. Either way, we're going out to dinner and having a nice time, but who's paying? This playful challenge is often the incentive clients need to stop procrastinating and finally finish their estate plan.

Don't be the person who puts off creating an estate plan year after year until an unexpected tragedy occurs and it's too late. Find someone to hold you accountable to a deadline and get it done sooner rather than later.

At this point, you may be thinking, "I thought this was a financial planning book... Why are we talking about estate planning?" Financial planning is about more than just an investment portfolio. Understanding the bigger picture allows us to put together a better retirement plan based on your goals.

Furthermore, when someone passes away, Uncle Sam usually gets involved. Combining estate planning and retirement planning allows us to make decisions that minimize how much of your wealth you and your heirs will lose to taxes.

Tax preparers, CPAs, and accountants are what I like to call "historians for the IRS". Their job is to put numbers in boxes that describe what you did last year. Meanwhile, a financial advisor's job is to look into the future and determine how we can reduce those numbers.

Let's do an activity that we often use with our clients. I want you to write the following six statements on index cards and then rank them from 1-6, with 1 being the highest priority. Then, have your spouse do the same. For "Other," write something you think is missing from this list.

- Maximize heirs' inheritance
- Maximize current lifestyle
- Never run out of money
- Leave an uncluttered legacy
- Minimize income taxes
- Other

Often, when spouses do this, they may discover they have different priorities. For example, husband and wife, Joe and Mary, complete this exercise. When they share their cards, they find that Joe's priority is to "maximize current lifestyle," while Mary's priority is to "maximize heirs' inheritance." Since these priorities are at odds with each other—the more the couple maximizes their current lifestyle, the less inheritance there will be for their heirs–they'll need to have conversations about their priorities with a financial advisor to build a financial plan that finds a compromise both spouses can be comfortable with.

Estate planning is one of the most overlooked parts of preparing for retirement, but I've found that people experience an immense sense of relief once they put an estate plan in place.

Estate and retirement planning doesn't have to be complicated. In fact, you can take care of retirement and estate planning in just two hours a year. Yes, that's right—two hours a year to build and maintain a plan to secure your financial future and remove any worry and uncertainty about money. Once those two hours are over, you can stop thinking about your financial plan and get back to enjoying your life.

My goal for this book is to simplify all the information you need to think about when building a successful retirement and estate plan. With this information in hand, you'll have clarity and be equipped to confidently walk into a meeting with a financial advisor. Once you've taken the time to create your plan with a professional, it should only take two hours a year to maintain and adjust your plan, ensuring you're always on track for the future you envision, even if your circumstances change.

At Hasenberg Financial Group, we accomplish this using the DCAC model. With this model, we have a one-hour meeting every six months to review and update your financial plan. We cycle through D, C, and A meeting types within a two-year period, meaning that for each two-year period, you'll have one D meeting, one A meeting, and two C meetings.

> **Our Model: The DCAC System**
>
> **D**eath and Distribution Review Meeting (6 months)
>
> **C**omprehensive Review Meeting (12 months)
>
> **A**sset Protection Meeting (18 months)
>
> **C**omprehensive Review Meeting (24 months)

In the Death and Distribution (D) meeting, we review and update your estate plan. If you were to die tomorrow, what would happen to your assets? If you're unhappy with any of the results, we update your plan to ensure your wishes are fulfilled.

This meeting is important because estate planning is not set in stone. Your estate plan must adapt to fit the shifting needs of your family. Each birth, death, divorce, or marriage among your loved ones may change the needs of your estate plan. For example, when your first grandchild is born, you may want to update your estate plan to fund his or her education. On the other hand, if there's a rift in your family and a family member starts making bad decisions, you may want to remove this person from your estate plan until they straighten up.

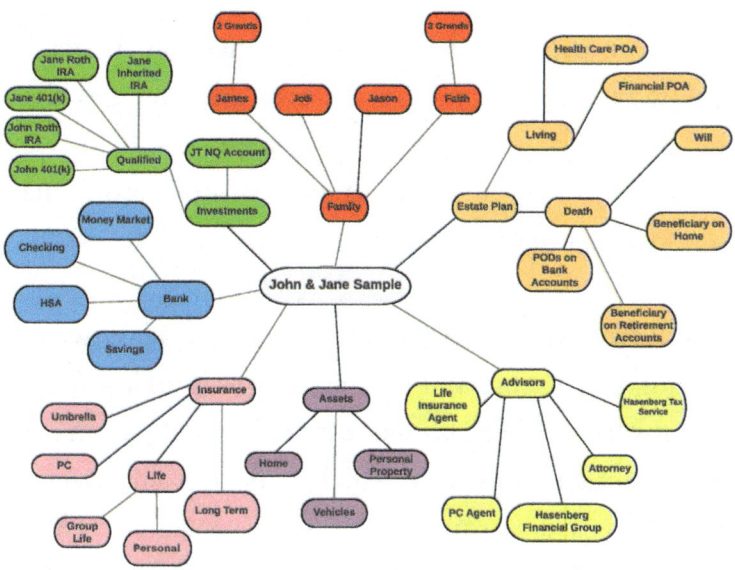

We'll show you a mind map that shows your current estate plan, your major assets, insurances, bank accounts, investment accounts, and advisors that you work with. The numbers are removed so that you can easily show your family members your estate plan without telling them the exact financial details—unless you choose to. The purpose of this mind map is to have a line of communication between you and the next generation about your estate and what will happen to it when you're gone.

During this meeting, we'll also look at tax strategies in regards to your estate plan. Is there anything we can change this year to ensure your heirs get to keep more of your estate and the government gets to keep less?

In the Comprehensive Review (C) meeting, which occurs annually, we discuss your goals and any changes that may have taken place, update your net worth statement (we call it an asset map) and your retirement planning target map. We also perform a market and tax review.

In the Asset Protection (A) meeting, we discuss what could go wrong in your life and put safeguards in place. We explore questions like, "What happens if you or your spouse die?" or "What happens if you get sued?" and develop strategies to protect your assets from each worst-case scenario. We review your property and casualty insurance, life insurance, disability insurance, and long-term care insurance. We review identity theft risks and stress test your investment portfolio.

Six months later, we have another C meeting.

That's the DCAC process—all accomplished in just two meetings a year so you can spend less time worrying about your finances and more time enjoying your life.

After two meetings per year for the first two years, we then start the cycle over again. In our experience, after the completion of the first full DCAC cycle, the D and A meetings often become optional. We always offer them, but unless changes have taken place, most of our clients feel happy with their plans.

Please note that the C meetings are critically important to have on an annual basis, and we don't like to think of them as optional. In our office, we believe that if you haven't met with your advisor in the last two years, you become a customer instead of a client. Clients tend to have more successful retirements than customers, so we really emphasize the importance of meeting at least annually.

But before you're ready to begin the DCAC process and simplify your financial planning to just two hours a year, we're going to unpack the most essential information you need to know about building a retirement and estate plan.

In the rest of this book, we'll cover:

- **What You Have and Where You Have It (Chapter 3):** Before we can create a plan, we need to take inventory of your current financial situation. This chapter will show you the process of creating an asset map that allows you to see your finances at a glance, which will be important when making decisions about retirement, tax planning, and estate planning. I'll also share four crucial tools that will ensure your family has the financial information they need to manage your estate if you pass away.

- **Knowing Your Number (Chapter 4):** So, how much do you really need to retire? We'll demystify this complex question and share the elements that make up your retirement portfolio. You'll also read about the three stages of retirement and how they interact with inflation. Understanding your number gives you a clear target when creating your plan.

- **The 12 Steps to Financial Independence (Chapter 5):** How should you manage your money throughout your life to set yourself up for financial independence? We've created a simple twelve-step system to help you prioritize how you save, invest, and pay off debt.

- **What is an Estate Plan (Chapter 6):** In this chapter, we'll cover the basics of estate planning and help you understand why estate planning is crucial. You'll have an opportunity to reflect on your goals for estate planning, both for when you're alive and after you're gone. Since tomorrow is never promised, having an estate plan is essential to ensure your wishes are carried out if you die or become incapacitated.

- **Planning for Incapacity (Chapter 7):** Who will make medical and financial decisions for you if you're incapacitated? What are the essential tools you need to implement to ensure your wishes are carried out? You don't want to leave these decisions up to chance. This chapter will share how you can prepare yourself and your loved ones for potential incapacity.

- **What Happens if You Die Without an Estate Plan (Chapter 8):** To help you grasp the importance of estate planning, we'll walk you through what happens when a person dies without an estate plan, including what happens when an estate goes through probate. Then, we'll share how you can avoid probate and spare your loved ones the stress and uncertainty of the process.

- **Wills and Trusts (Chapter 9):** We'll cover the six most common types of estate documents so you comprehend the tools available to you when creating an estate plan. We'll also discuss the importance of fitting your estate planning strategy to the unique needs of your family.

- **Taxes (Chapter 10):** Everyone's favorite topic! When creating a retirement or estate plan, we can't forget to account for how taxes will affect you. We'll explore the types of taxes your heirs will face after your death and address how to minimize your tax burden. The goal is to (legally, of course) reduce the portion of your estate that the IRS keeps so your heirs, whether family members or a favorite charity, will keep more of your hard-earned assets.

- **Long Term Care and Nursing Homes (Chapter 11):** As we get older, we all have to prepare for the possibility that we'll need long term care or a nursing home. As much as 50% of the population may need to go into a nursing home at some point, so it's important to ensure you have a plan to pay for your care. In this chapter, we'll also break down what you need to know about Medicaid.

- **Your Financial Team (Chapter 12):** Now that you're ready to create your financial plan, how do you find an advisor who can become your trusted, long-term financial coach? How do you distinguish a trustworthy advisor from a salesperson who doesn't have your best interests at heart? What other professionals do you need to have on your financial team? How can you build your own "family office," even if you're not ultra-wealthy?

With all of this information in hand, you'll be ready to handle it on your own or walk into a meeting with an advisor and begin your financial planning journey.

Are you ready to secure your financial future? Read on…

CHAPTER 3

What You Have and Where You Have It

"We believe a financial picture is worth a thousand decisions."

— Asset Map

Do you know what you have?

Before we can create your financial plan, we need to understand what you have. To accomplish this, we guide our clients through the process of creating a tool we call an "asset map".

There are two main benefits to creating an asset map:

1) You'll get clarity about what you have in an organized manner.

2) You'll be better equipped to make informed financial decisions.

The asset map lists each spouse's current and future income streams, individually owned assets, jointly owned assets, and applicable insurance policies. The map totals each spouse's assets and the couple's joint assets. We begin each client meeting by updating the asset map so we have the most accurate view of a couple's entire financial picture.

Before we dive into the rest of the book, take a moment to review your assets and inventory what you have:

Protection Plan
- Group life insurance information (amount & cost)
- Personal life insurance information (last statement & policy)
- Health insurance information or Medicare Supplement information
- Disability insurance information (Coverage amount & cost)
- Long Term Care (Nursing Home) Insurance Information
- Auto & Home Insurance (Declaration Page & Policy)
- Identity Theft Insurance

Estate Plan
- Will
- Power of Attorney
- Trust documents
- Marital Property Agreement
- Transfer on Death Deed

Retirement Plan
- Latest IRA statements
- Latest 401K statements
- Latest Roth IRA statements
- Latest 403b/TSA statement
- Latest pension statements
- Latest 457/Deferred Comp statement

Income Taxes
- Last 2 years income tax returns (state and federal)

Personal Property
- Primary mortgage information (Debt balance, % rate, payment)
- Secondary mortgage information (Debt balance, % rate, payment)
- Credit Card statements
- Other personal debt information (Debt balance, % rate, payment)

Investment Plan
- Savings & checking statement from bank
- Bank statements listing CD balances & rates
- Latest annuity statement
- Latest mutual fund statements (preferably statements from the investment companies themselves, not a printout from the internet)
- Savings bond information

For a complete data-gathering checklist, visit www.hasenberginc.com/book.

Additional Information You Should Have Consolidated

There's nothing worse than waiting by your deceased parents' mailbox for weeks, hoping the cell phone bill shows up, and praying that they didn't opt for electronic billing—because you don't know the password to log in to their email and cancel the service. What if you can't get into their account to turn off the billing, and payments keep being automatically deducted from their bank account?

What if something happens to you or your spouse? Could your spouse or heirs easily access everything they need?

We've developed many simple tools to help our clients through this process. Below are a few examples, but you can find the complete checklist at www.hasenberginc.com/book.

1. **Digital Vault**

    Create a digital vault so you can access digital copies of important documents from anywhere. One of our clients, for instance, lost his passport while traveling internationally. Thanks to his digital vault, he was able to show officials a copy of his passport and exit the country.

2. **Household Expenses Document**
   In many households, one spouse handles the finances while the other remains uninvolved. If the spouse who typically handles the finances passes away first, the other spouse will be left not knowing what to do. To prevent this problem, create a Household Expenses Document that lists each household expense and how it is paid, along with any other best practices your spouse would need to know about handling your household's finances.

3. **In Case of Emergency Key**
   Place a USB drive on your keychain that contains important documents and information about your health history. If you have a health emergency and aren't able to communicate, this USB can provide crucial information to healthcare professionals and change your standard of care.

4. **A Binder Full of Essential Documents**
   We live in a world in which technology is advancing rapidly. Though we use a lot of technology during the financial planning process, there are certain things you might want to have printed. We create a binder for each client that keeps all of the important documents in one place for easy reference. Having physical copies

on hand makes it easy for you to take action and gives you a clear picture of what you have.

5. **Estate Organizer Document**
   A list of things that your heirs must-do if you pass away. By completing this document for them, your wishes are more likely to be known and followed.

Preparing these items ensures your loved ones have everything they need to handle your finances after you're gone, sparing them the stress of sorting through a disorganized mess in your absence.

CHAPTER 4

Know Your Number

So, how do you determine your number?

As a rule of thumb, each year you'll need 80% of your pre-retirement income.

Why not 100%? During your working years, you set aside part of your income for retirement, but once you're retired, you no longer need to save for it.

If your pre-retirement income is $100,000, your ideal post-retirement income may need to be $80,000 or higher.

Debt is an important part of this equation. We believe the richest people in the world are not those with the most money, but those who need the least. So, less debt in retirement is best.

Retirement can be as simple as each spouse's Social Security, possibly a pension, and income from an investment portfolio. If these accounts provide 80% of your pre-retirement income, you are at your number.

You may be wondering, "What about inflation? Why doesn't my retirement income rise over time as the cost of living rises?"

To answer this question, we need to look at the three stages of retirement:

1. The "Go-Go" Years (60s)
2. The "Slow-Go" Years (70s)
3. The "No-Go" Years (80s+)

In your 60s, you'll likely have the most energy and be excited for retirement. During this decade, you'll take the most vacations, attend exciting events like music festivals or sports games, and travel often to visit family.

In your 70s, you'll still be active, but your enthusiasm for travel may begin to wane. You may prefer local trips rather than international ones and attend fewer events as they become more exhausting.

In your 80s and beyond, you'll likely stay close to home as your energy levels decrease. This can still be a fulfilling stage of life, but you are less likely to spend money on things like international travel or sporting activities that you enjoyed when you were younger.

So even as the cost of living rises with inflation, your personal expenses may decrease as you age and become less active. That doesn't mean other things don't change. Other expenses, such as healthcare and medications, may increase in your 80s. But we've found that people's cost of living in retirement tends to stay about the same year after year. Expenses will always be there, but your priorities will shift with each decade.

Understanding Your Portfolio

You may feel that you need a large amount of money to retire, but your expenses may not be as high as you think they are.

A common rule of thumb is to draw 4% from your portfolio each year of retirement. For example, if your pre-retirement income is $100,000, your desired post-retirement income may be $80,000. If you and your spouse's Social Securities and pensions add up to $40,000, then you may want to draw the other $40,000 from your investment portfolio. At a 4% withdrawal rate, you would need an investment portfolio of around $1,000,000.

We believe that if you withdraw 4% or less from your portfolio, you're unlikely to run out of money. In fact, your account may even grow which helps with future inflation. If you withdraw 4 - 7% from your portfolio, you probably won't run out of money, but inflation in the future may become an issue. However, if you take out more than 7% of your account balance per year, it's only a matter of time until you run out of money. So, using the below-referenced example, you can see that withdrawal rates and account balances change often, which is why an annual review is so important.

Year	June 30 Balance	Withdrawals	Withdrawal Rate
2016	$495,896	$36,000	7.26%
2017	$486,060	$48,020	9.88%
2018	$459,942	$38,715	8.42%
2019	$444,893	$19,094	4.29%
2020	$450,806	$2,520	0.56%
2021	$610,148	$23,496	3.85%
2022	$461,702	$24,800	5.37%
2023	$437,095	$20,741	4.75%

Average: 5.55%

Less than 4%
4% - 7%
Greater than 7%

- Withdrawing too much money in retirement limits how log your savings last.
- A prudent withdrawal (3-5%, adjusted and revisited annually) can increase the probabilities of success.
- Other factors that may affect the longevity of assets include the investment mix, fees, life expectancy, sequence of returns.
- These figures are for illustrative purposes only and do not represent any particular investment of reflect investment fees, expenses or taxes.
- Past performance is no guarantee of future results.

Since your portfolio supplies such a large part of your retirement income, it should be carefully managed. We use a lot of different tools and modeling to fine-tune the diversification and risk exposure of our clients' investments.

This is something you need to work on with an advisor, and this is why the right advisor can make a big difference. But for this book, I just want you to understand the big picture.

We've developed investment models and have trading discretion. If the market starts to deteriorate, we can adjust the risk in our clients' portfolios. In contrast, many of our competitors operate with non-discretionary accounts, meaning the advisor must contact the client to make changes. They may start with their largest clients first, and by the time they get to you, the market might have already shifted, making it too late.

Some investment firms consider adjusting a client's portfolio from 60% equities and 40% bonds to 58% equities and 42% bonds a big adjustment. However, to us, this minor shift might not even be worth mentioning. Our portfolio risk adjustments can go from 60/40 to 10/90 or even to 100/0 depending on the account and current market conditions. Our goal as a firm is to participate in much of the upside of the market while minimizing the downside of the market to the best of our abilities. Of course, past performance is no guarantee of the future, but these are the goals of our firm for our clients investment portfolios.

Ultimately, "knowing your number" is specific to you and your family's unique situation. It's important to work through an advisor to navigate this journey.

Remember, "Personal finance is more personal than it is finance."

CHAPTER 5

12 Steps to Financial Independence

When you get to the end of the month and have money left over, what should you do with it? Should you put it in a retirement account? An education fund? Should it go towards a cash reserve or paying down debt?

To make this decision easier, we've created the 12 Steps to Financial Independence. These steps, primarily for those who have not yet retired, aid with prioritizing how you allocate your assets. You can start this process in your twenties and continue through retirement and beyond. Please note: it's important to *complete each step in order*.

The 12 Steps to Financial Independence

Step 1: $1,500 cash into a 1st-tier reserve
Step 2: Pay off >6% tax equivalent non-house debt

Step 3: Participate in the matching portion of the retirement plan, if available
Step 4: Save 3 months of expenses into a 2nd tier cash reserve
Step 5: Fund 10% of income into retirement plans.
- Roth IRA if in 12% tax bracket or lower
- Pre-tax if above 12% bracket
Step 6: Fund 529 plan to maximum deductible level (if college is a goal)
Step 7: Pay off <6% tax equivalent debt, except for house
Step 8: Save additional 3 months of expenses into 3rd tier cash reserve
Step 9: Increase retirement savings rate to 15% of income
Step 10: Build non-qualified investment portfolio of 1.5x annual income
Step 11: Pay off house
Step 12: Set up legacy plan

Identify where you stand in the twelve steps. You may have completed them out of order. In that case, go back and complete any skipped steps. For example, if you've completed steps 1, 2, 3, 5, and 7, we recommend putting steps 5 and 7 on hold until you complete step 4. Then, you can continue to proceed in order.

Once you've completed these twelve steps, you'll be well on your way to financial independence.

For a free PDF list of these 12 steps, go to www.hasenberginc.com/book

Now, let's take a closer look at each step:

Step 1: Prioritizing Cash Reserves

Starting with a cash reserve is crucial. The first tier of $1,500 is your immediate buffer for unexpected expenses like car repairs, minor medical bills, or urgent home repairs. This small yet significant cushion prevents you from relying on credit cards or loans, which can lead to accumulating high-interest debt.

Step 2: High-Interest Debt Repayment

Next, addressing high-interest debt is vital. Non-mortgage debts with interest rates above 6% can quickly snowball, making it harder to achieve financial independence. Prioritize paying off these debts to free up cash flow and reduce the overall interest paid over time. High-interest debt, such as credit card balances, can be financially crippling and should be eliminated as quickly as possible.

Step 3: Maximizing Employer Retirement Plans

Participating in an employer-sponsored retirement plan, especially when there is a matching contribution, is a strategic move. The matching contribution is essentially free money, providing an immediate return on your investment. For example, if your employer matches up to 4% of your salary, contribute at least that amount to take full advantage of the match. This step helps you build your retirement savings early, leveraging compound interest over the long term.

Step 4: Building a Robust Cash Reserve

Once you've secured the employer match, focus on building a more substantial cash reserve, equivalent to three months of living expenses. This second tier of cash reserves provides a more significant safety net against larger financial disruptions like job loss or major health issues. A well-funded cash reserve can prevent you from liquidating investments or incurring debt during emergencies.

Step 5: Strategic Retirement Savings

After establishing a solid emergency fund, increase your retirement contributions. If you're in a lower tax bracket, consider a Roth IRA, which allows for tax-free withdrawals in retirement. If you're in a higher tax bracket, pre-tax contributions to traditional retirement accounts can provide immediate tax benefits. This step ensures that you're consistently saving a portion of your income for your future, with tax strategies tailored to your current financial situation.

Step 6: Education Funding (if applicable)

If saving for a child's education is a priority, contribute to a 529 plan up to the maximum deductible level. These plans offer tax advantages and can be a valuable tool for managing future education costs. However, it's essential to balance education savings with retirement contributions, as your retirement needs should take precedence.

Step 7: Low-Interest Debt Repayment

Paying off low-interest debt, such as certain student loans or auto loans, comes next. While these debts are less burdensome due to their lower interest rates, eliminating them still improves your financial stability and frees up cash flow for other investments.

Step 8: Third Tier Cash Reserve

Expanding your cash reserve to cover six months of expenses provides an additional layer of security, particularly useful in times of prolonged financial uncertainty. This third tier ensures you can weather extended periods of reduced income without compromising your financial goals.

Step 9: Increase Retirement Savings

Increasing your retirement savings rate to 15% of your income is the next logical step. This higher savings rate accelerates your progress towards financial independence, allowing your investments to grow more significantly over time.

Step 10: Non-Qualified Investment Portfolio (a.k.a. Gap Money)

Building a non-qualified investment portfolio that equals 1.5 times your annual income diversifies your financial strategy beyond retirement accounts. These investments can include stocks, bonds, real estate, or other assets that generate returns and build wealth. This can also provide assets for the gap between your retirement and age 65 for health insurance purposes.

Step 11: Achieving Debt-Free Homeownership

Paying off your mortgage is a significant milestone. Owning your home outright reduces your monthly expenses and increases your financial security. It also allows you to allocate more funds towards investments and other financial goals.

Step 12: Legacy Planning

Finally, setting up a legacy plan ensures that your wealth is preserved and passed on according to your wishes. This step involves estate planning, creating wills, and possibly setting up trusts to manage your assets and provide for your loved ones after your passing.

Customizing Your Financial Journey

The twelve steps are a helpful framework, but personal circumstances often require adjustments. For example, if you receive a windfall, such as an inheritance or a large bonus, you might skip ahead to fund a significant portion of your retirement accounts or fund your Non-Qualified Investment Portfolio (Step 10). Flexibility is key and you should work with a financial advisor to tailor these steps to your unique situation.

I had a client in his forties who had recently received a substantial bonus from work. He was trying to decide whether to use the bonus to pay off his mortgage or invest it. After discussing his long-term goals and current financial situation we realized he was past step 9, so we decided to split the bonus. Half went towards the mortgage to reduce future interest payments, and the other half was invested in a diversified portfolio to take advantage of potential market growth. This balanced approach best aligned with his risk tolerance and financial objectives based on our conversation and personalized plan.

The 12 Steps to Financial Independence provide a comprehensive roadmap to achieving financial stability and freedom. By following these steps and adapting them to your individual needs, you can confidently navigate your financial journey and build a secure future for yourself and your family.

Of course, while the twelve steps are a good template for a general audience, sitting down individually with an advisor is a better option. I went through this process with a client in his late thirties who was selling his house. He had some student loan debt with an interest rate that was greater than 6%. We discussed the difference between good debt and bad debt.

Bad debt is associated with things that are decreasing in value, like credit cards and cars, while good debt is tied to things that will increase in value, like education and real estate. His student loan debt was good debt because it was an investment in his education that would eventually enable him to earn a higher salary.

We decided to deviate from the 12 steps and not pay off his student loans, even though they were above 6%, because he would easily be able to pay them off in the future when his income increased. Instead, we kept the money liquid so that he could put a down payment on a new home if he wanted to. Everyone's situation is different, and these 12 steps serve as a helpful guideline, not a hard-and-fast rule. An advisor will help you personalize your plan to fit your unique situation and needs.

One final note: In the 12 steps, retirement savings come before children's education. Remember, you can get a loan for education, but you cannot get a loan for retirement.

CHAPTER 6

What is an Estate Plan (and Why Do You Need It)?

When I give seminars, I ask people to raise their hands if there are any insurance agents, investment advisors, bankers, accountants, or lawyers in the room. Usually, nobody raises their hand.

Then, I say, "The reason I ask is because I'm going to pick on all of those professionals today. And I just want to know who I'm picking on."

Then, I tell this story…

A friend of mine got pulled over for a minor traffic violation. When the police officer came up to the window to see her driver's license, she also handed him her concealed carry license. She said, "Just so you know, I have a small pistol in my purse."

The police officer said, "Thanks for letting me know."

Then, my friend said, "Also, just so you know, I carry a .357 in the console, I've got a .44 magnum in the glove box, and I keep a shotgun in the trunk.

The police officer said, "Ma'am, who are you afraid of?"

She said, "Absolutely nobody."

When it comes to estate planning, what are you afraid of? Are you worried Uncle Sam will take all your money? Are you afraid that a nursing home will drain your finances? Are you concerned with leaving your kids a financial mess? Do you worry about losing your money through investments? What fear brought you to this book and kept you turning the pages in search of an answer?

My mission is to give guidance that helps people to enjoy life more and worry less. I want you to be able to say, like my friend, "I'm afraid of nobody"—because you know you're prepared for any financial threat to your retirement.

> **Disclaimer: I'm not a lawyer, and the information in this book isn't legal advice—just information.**

Over the last thirty years, I've met with thousands of households, and found that most people share common goals:

- They want their estate to be distributed according to their desires, not the court's.
- They want to avoid taxes as much as they can.
- They want to avoid probate.
- They want their loved ones to make their medical and financial decisions if they cannot.
- They want to protect their assets from being consumed by nursing home costs.
- They want to keep their family and financial matters private.

You might share all of these goals or just one or two. No matter what your goals are, an estate plan can help you achieve them.

What is an estate plan? It's a reflection of your goals, detailing how you want things handled in the event of your death or incapacity.

Who needs an estate plan? The short answer is: everybody. But an estate plan is especially important if:

1) You handle the finances in your relationship and want to make sure your spouse can handle them if you pass away first.

   My wife knows that I handle the finances in our household, and she once told me, "If something happened to you, I wouldn't know what to do."

   Knowing that other couples face this same fear, I created organizers, tools, and checklists to ensure both spouses have all the necessary information in case the spouse who handles the finances passes away first. To access this free resource, go to www.hasenberginc.com/book.

2) You own a business. Business owners have their own set of estate planning challenges. If you got hit by a bus tomorrow, what would happen to your company? Also, do you own a business or a practice? (We will talk more about this in an upcoming chapter…)

3) You're wealthy. If you have a large amount of wealth, an estate plan is crucial because you may face high estate taxes.

Estate planning has two phases: while you're alive and after you're dead.

While you're alive, we have to deal with your health and your finances. Everyone over 18 needs to have a healthcare directive and a durable financial power of attorney.

One of the most important decisions in the "while you're alive" phase of estate planning is choosing the best person to serve as your power of attorney.

Typically, if you're married, you list your spouse as your first choice for power of attorney. When you list a secondary person, or a first person if you're single, you have more factors to consider.

One is your heir's occupation. For example, if your son is a CPA and your daughter is an RN, it makes sense to have the CPA be your financial power of attorney and have the RN be the healthcare power of attorney.

You may also want to consider geography. If one of your children lives nearby while another is across the country, it's practical to choose the one who's close for power of attorney duties. After all, it would be challenging for a distant child to check your mailbox for the Visa bill.

Another consideration when selecting the financial power of attorney is choosing someone who has the financial incentive to not mess up. A child who is going to inherit your money is likely to make better decisions with your assets than a friend who has no financial stake in the outcome.

I'm often asked if it's okay for the healthcare and financial power of attorneys to be the same person. The answer is yes, that's often fine. Another common question is if it's okay to name two people. The answer is yes, but it may not be a good idea. When the surgeon comes to the waiting room to ask a question, having two people arguing is not a good situation. Consider naming one person, than if that person is unwilling or unable, listing out a second person.

Likewise, after death, your trustee or executor of your estate should be someone who has a vested interest in it. Your heir will take more time to make sure the house is in proper shape when they sell it than someone who doesn't have a financial benefit in doing so.

After your death, estate planning gets a little more complicated. It involves managing wills, probate, taxes, trusts, and insurance. We'll cover these topics later in the book. For now, let's turn our attention to planning for incapacity.

CHAPTER 7

Planning for Incapacity

What's the first thing people think about when they think of incapacity?

The inability to make decisions.

Usually, people associate incapacity with Alzheimer's, dementia, and strokes.

But incapacity can happen to anyone at any time.

If you've ever had a surgical procedure in a hospital and been under anesthesia, you've been incapacitated.

You don't have to be elderly or unable to make your own medical decisions.

That's why having an estate plan in place is crucial.

Without the proper documentation in place, you may have to go through a guardianship process, which involves the court and lawyers and can quickly get expensive and time-consuming. Sometimes, the court-appointed guardian might not be who you wanted it to be.

You can avoid this by having healthcare directives and powers of attorney in place.

Here are the essential healthcare directives you need:

- Living Will – Puts your instructions in writing
- Durable Power of Attorney for Healthcare (Healthcare Proxy) - Lets you designate an agent to make decisions on your behalf
- Do Not Resuscitate (DNR) Order - Directs that resuscitative measures be withheld or withdrawn. In other words: "Keep me alive by machines or pull the plug?"

Not all types of healthcare directives are valid in every state, so be sure to execute those that will be effective where you live.

You'll also want to establish property management tools to determine how financial decisions will be made if you're incapacitated. These include:

- Joint Ownership - A joint owner has the same access to property as you do
- Durable Power of Attorney (DPOA) - Lets you designate an agent to make decisions on your behalf
- Living Trust - Allows a successor trustee to take over management of trust property

Joint ownership is one way to manage incapacity but it can lead to problems. Say an elderly mother has a joint checking account with her daughter to help pay bills. If the daughter gets sued or divorced, the assets in the checking account could be at risk. Legally, the account is jointly owned so the money that the mother uses to pay her bills could end up in the hands of her daughter's new ex-husband.

The other problem with joint ownership is that if you die, ownership takes precedence. All of a sudden, all the money in the checking account that was supposed to go to all of the heirs becomes owned by the joint owner. If your daughter is the joint owner of your checking account, and you want the money divided equally between your three children, you'd better hope that your daughter would do the right thing and share the money with her siblings. But after you're gone, without legal protections in place, there's no guarantee she'll follow your wishes—and if she does, she might face gift tax issues.

An alternative to joint ownership may be to be a signer on the account. This allows your daughter to help write your checks without owning the account. Check with your bank or credit union to learn your options.

A better way to handle incapacity is a durable financial power of attorney, which allows someone to make decisions on your behalf if you're incapacitated–without owning your assets.

If you have a trust, the trust document can specify who your contingent trustee would be if you become incapacitated.

Planning for the possibility of incapacity is crucial because you never know when or if it could happen. Once it does, it's too late to go back in time and ensure your wishes will be protected.

Do you want to ensure that your wishes are protected and that your family members know what to do, or do you want to leave it to chance?

CHAPTER 8

What Happens If You Die Without an Estate Plan?

In this chapter, we'll explore what happens if someone dies without an estate plan.

First, ownership takes precedence. If someone has joint ownership of assets with the deceased, the assets immediately pass to them without going to probate. For example, if you and your spouse have a joint checking account, when you pass away, your spouse can take the death certificate to the bank and change the ownership from a joint account into an individual account.

After ownership, we consider beneficiaries. If an insurance or retirement account has a beneficiary on it, the account will automatically pass to the beneficiary without going to probate. Beneficiaries take precedence over anything written in the estate plan, meaning no matter what the will says, the account will pass to the listed beneficiary.

Go to your file cabinet and pull out the insurance policy you bought years ago. Take a look at the beneficiaries. Usually, if you're married, your spouse will be the primary beneficiary, and the contingent beneficiary might be your children, with the policy specifying an even split between them. This is a problem because the insurance company doesn't know how many kids you have. Your intended beneficiaries should be listed with birth dates and Social Security numbers.

Sometimes, when people check old insurance policies, they may find that an ex-spouse is listed or that they bought their policy before one of their children was born. It's crucial to make sure your beneficiaries are correct because this will override anything you have written in a will.

If an asset doesn't have joint ownership or beneficiaries and/or trust ownership, it will likely go to probate. If you don't have a will, your state of residence probably has one for you. It will likely say that if you pass away, everything goes to your spouse. If you both pass away, it's split evenly between the kids. If you don't have kids and your parents are alive, it goes to your parents. If your parents have passed away, it goes to your brothers and sisters.

What happens if you pass away and don't have a living spouse, kids, parents, or siblings? Your assets might go to the state education fund. The ironic part? The state educational system usually doesn't teach much about personal finance...

For married couples, it often becomes survival of the fittest. What I mean is that if a married couple doesn't have a will and the husband passes away, all the assets might automatically transfer into the wife's name.

Then, if the wife passes away and the couple doesn't have kids, the assets will go to the wife's parents, who might be going into a nursing home. So, it's possible that all of the assets may go to one side of the family rather than being divided evenly between each spouse's family.

How Does Probate Work?

I want you to understand how probate works so you understand why you never want your heirs to go through it.

Have you ever helped anyone go through probate or known anyone who has? When I ask this question in seminars, I ask how long it took from the person's death to the end of the probate process. The average is around 13 months. I've seen it go as fast as six weeks or as long as ten years and counting.

The initial steps in the probate process are:

1. A petition is filed in probate court
2. Notices are published in the newspaper
3. Hearings are held before the probate court
4. The will is approved
5. A personal representative is appointed
6. Creditors are notified

> **Note:** When your assets are going to probate, your creditors, meaning everyone you owe money to, are notified. Do you have a list of everyone you owe money to, including credit cards, IOU'S, debts, mortgages, and loans? If you don't, would your heirs be able to figure it out?

7. Assets are then appraised.

> **Note:** At death, appraisal is often a taxable event, and there are cost-basis reasons why things need to be appraised, especially appreciated assets like real estate, art, or collectibles that may have gone up in value. If the survivor decided to sell these assets, they would have to prove the cost basis for tax purposes.

8. An inventory of assets is prepared and filed.

> **Note:** The operative word here is filed, meaning the list of everything you own becomes public record! Isn't it interesting? We spend our entire

> lives not telling anyone how much money we have or where it is, and then when you die, if your estate goes through probate, it becomes public record.

9. Annual accountings are filed
10. Attorneys are paid
11. Estate taxes (if applicable) are paid
12. Income taxes are paid
13. Creditors are paid
14. A personal representative may be paid
15. Whatever is left is distributed to the family

(Notice how attorneys get paid before the government… Isn't that something? You can tell who probably made the rules.)

So that's the probate process. As you can see, there are a lot of steps, it takes a long time, and you have little control. You want to avoid probate at all costs.

How to Avoid Probate

There are a few ways to avoid probate:

- Joint ownership
- Beneficiaries
- TOD (Transfer On Death on brokerage accounts)
- POD (Payable On Death on bank accounts)

- Trusts
- Transfer On Death Deed for Real Estate

Another way of avoiding probate is to give your assets away while you're alive. The advantage to that is you get to see what your heirs do with the money. The downside about doing that is you get to see what your heirs do with the money...

One lesser-known method of avoiding probate is designating beneficiaries on real estate through what is called a Transfer on Death Deed. The reason most people don't know about this is that nobody gets paid to sell them. An attorney can make money on a $5,000 trust, but they don't make much money filing a $200 Transfer on Death Deed document.

It's important to note that this information is not intended as advice. My purpose in this book is simply to inform and educate you about common options. To get the best results, you'll need to meet with an advisor and assess your unique situation.

In the next chapter, we'll dive into the essential elements of an estate plan that can keep your assets out of probate.

CHAPTER 9

Wills and Trusts

What is a will? A will is a set of written instructions to tell probate court what to do with your assets. Yes, a will goes through probate.

A will is the cornerstone of an estate plan. It directs how your property will be distributed after your death. If you have minor children, it names their executor and guardian. It is written and signed by you in front of a witness.

Yet a will by itself isn't enough. If the beneficiaries on an account are wrong, a will can't override this mistake.

Recently, I saw a case where the beneficiary form on an account was filed wrong, so the estate had to go through probate. Despite the will clearly stating that the assets were to be divided 50/50 between the client's two sons, the presence of other beneficiaries listed in the will led to a complex, stressful probate process for the family.

So, although wills are the cornerstone of an estate plan, estate planning cannot stop at a will. In fact, we believe that everyone should have a will, but our goal is not to use it because all of the assets were structured to avoid probate.

A trust is a versatile estate planning tool that can protect against incapacity, avoid probate, and minimize taxes. It allows for the professional management of your assets and provides safeguards for minor children, elderly parents, and other beneficiaries.

Basically, trusts are another type of ownership that says who can make decisions if you cannot and tells them what to do with your assets after your death.

Most trusts are revocable, allowing changes during your lifetime. Irrevocable trusts are less common. One of the reasons I don't like irrevocable trusts is because the government can change the rules (for example, with taxes), but an irrevocable trust is just that: irrevocable. If the laws change, you won't be able to change your irrevocable trust to take advantage of new opportunities or avoid potential problems.

There are six common types of estate documents:

1. **The Basic Will aka the "I Love You" Will**
   A basic will is a legal document that explains how you want your property to be divided after your death. This simple will names the beneficiaries you want to inherit your property, and it also names a will executor, who will carry out the wishes in the will. If you have minor children or pets, you can name guardians for them. Often, a simple will is nicknamed the "I Love You" will because most people tend to leave their entire estate to their spouse. A will must be signed in front of a witness.

2. **Will with Contingent Trust**
   A will with contingent trust is usually used in cases where someone has a child who is a minor. This will create a trust that goes into effect after your death, with a trustee appointed to manage the assets and use them for the care and education of the child, listing asset distribution amounts at different ages. If you have heirs who are receiving Social Security disability, you may want to consider a Special Needs trust so that an inheritance from you doesn't disqualify them from receiving benefits.

3. **Marital Property Agreement**

   A marital property agreement is an agreement between spouses that says what's his is hers and what's hers is his. This agreement is sometimes used to fix titling issues associated with some assets as well as have some large tax ramifications in the future if assets are sold. If you live in a community property state like Wisconsin, I have not seen any downside to having this document. I'm not sure about its effectiveness in non-community property states, so be sure to consult with an attorney and a CPA in your local area.

4. **The Pour-Over Will**

   A pour-over will dictates that your remaining assets will automatically transfer to a previously established trust upon your death.

5. **Living Trust Without Tax Planning**

   A living trust holds your assets while you're alive and distributes them after your death.

6. **QTIP (Qualified Terminable Interest Property) Trust**

   A QTIP trust sets aside resources for a surviving spouse. Typically, your spouse receives income for the rest of his or her life, and the assets are distributed to listed heirs upon the second death. This is a popular tool used in second marriages to protect assets for descendants.

90+% of the population can have their needs met by a combination of one to six of these solutions. I've personally had all six of these documents at some point in my life. Some people need one, some people need two, and some people need all six.

I do want to point out that less than 10% of our clients have trusts. The average person usually doesn't need one, but there are cases in which it makes sense. Trusts are sometimes preferred when there are many beneficiaries or if you have the wayward heir. As a parent, you always hope the wayward heir comes back into the family, and if they do, it's easier to change one trust than all of your accounts individually.

Everyone's situation is different. If it was simple and everyone needed the same thing, everyone would have their estate planning done. But reality is more complicated, so it's crucial to consult an expert who can help you determine which documents your unique situation requires.

Sometimes, there are alternative options to achieving financial goals. For example, my wife and I both have children from previous marriages. In blended families, it's common for assets to pass to the surviving spouse upon the first death, and then to their children after the second spouse's death, essentially disinheriting the first spouse's children.

We wanted to avoid this problem, so before we got married, we had a prenuptial agreement drawn up that largely dismisses community property laws and says that at death, premarital assets titled in my wife's name go to her children, assets titled in my name go to my children, and anything we accumulate during our marriage goes to each other upon first death, then upon second death, half goes to my children and half goes to hers.

This seemed like a good plan at the time, but we soon realized it had some issues. First, most of our premarital assets were in retirement accounts. By naming our children as beneficiaries of these accounts, they would be forced to pay income taxes on their inheritance within ten years, whereas a spouse would not be forced to do that.

Second, if one of us died today, what relationship might we have with the other spouse's children 30+ years from now? We love each other's children, but we don't know what things will be like decades into the future. When creating an estate plan, it's important to consider all the "what-ifs" about how your family dynamics and circumstances may change over the course of your life.

So, we decided to fix this problem with life insurance. I bought a proper amount of twenty-year term life insurance on each one of us and made our children the beneficiary of our policy. That way, upon first death, we know that our children are taken care of. We then changed the primary beneficiary of our retirement accounts to each other, so that as a spousal beneficiary, we wouldn't be forced into paying income taxes.

Taking it one step further, we then agreed that upon the second death, since our families were already taken care of with the life insurance proceeds, we would donate our retirement accounts to charity, essentially leaving the government out of the list of beneficiaries of our assets.

Given our ages, we only bought 20-year term insurance. So what happens in 20 years? We will figure it out then. Basically, we put a twenty-year bandage on our estate plan, and it makes me happy knowing the only loser in this plan would be the government.

This is only one example of the many ways estate planning can be tailored to meet the unique needs of each family–and the need to consider all the complexities of your family while creating your estate plan. What relationships with kids, step-kids, grandkids, your spouse, your ex-spouse, and your extended family do you need to consider? What complications and challenges do you face due to your family's distinct situation and relationships? How might these relationships change over decades?

When we meet with people having estate planning concerns, we give everyone an Estate Planning and Survivor's Checklist, an Estate Planning Checklist, and a Digital Vault Checklist. You can have these free resources by going to www.hasenberginc.com/book and requesting them.

There's no one-size-fits-all estate plan because every family is different.

The process of making these decisions can feel complex (because, let's face it, families are often complex), but completing your estate plan brings the reward of knowing that you'll provide for your loved ones after you're gone—and in the way you want to provide for them.

CHAPTER 10

Taxes

Have you seen the IRS's new tax form?

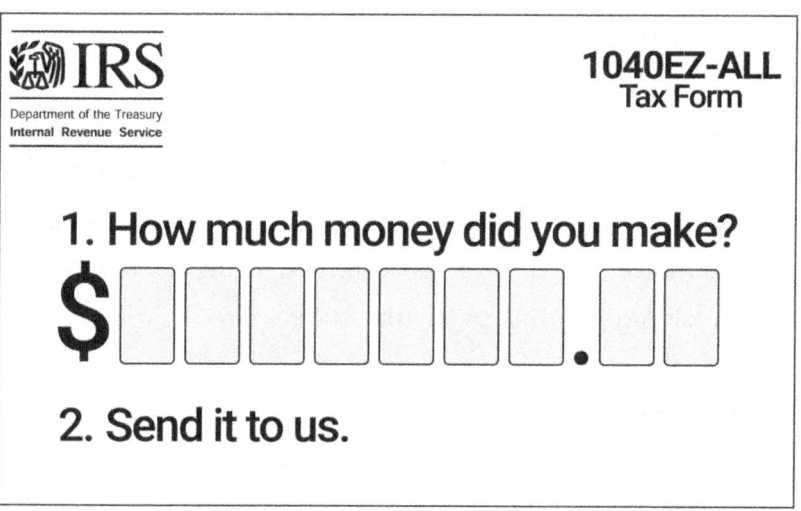

Just kidding, but sometimes, that's what it feels like…

A key part of estate planning is minimizing your taxes so that more of your estate can go to your heirs, and not to the IRS after you pass away.

There are primarily three types of federal taxes that may be imposed when property is transferred from one person to another either during life or at death. Referred to collectively as "transfer taxes," these taxes include:

- Federal gift tax: Imposed on transfers you make during your life
- Federal estate tax: Imposed on transfers made upon your death
- Income taxes: Imposed on distributions from tax-deferred accounts

We're going to discuss transfer taxes on the federal level only, but be aware that individual states may also impose their own transfer taxes, and they generally affect larger estates. It's important for you to get more information on the transfer taxes imposed by your particular state.

Federal Gift Tax

If you (the donor) transfer property to another person (the donee) during life, the transfer may be subject to gift tax. The reason for this gift tax is to prevent individuals from avoiding the estate tax by giving all their property away before they die.

The gift tax doesn't apply to every lifetime gift, however. For example, in 2024, you can give up to $18,000 to as many individuals as you want, gift tax-free, under the annual gift tax exclusion. The annual gift tax exclusion is indexed for inflation, so it may change in future years. Additionally, each individual has an exemption from all transfers (gifts and your estate) combined. In 2024, that estate tax exemption is $13.61 million for an individual and $27.22 million for a married couple.

It's important to note that if you go even a dollar over this $18,000, you will be subject to federal gift tax if the total lifetime gift exceeds the exclusion. So, even if you give someone $18,000 in cash and then buy them lunch or a birthday present, you are technically supposed to file a gift tax return.

A common estate planning strategy to minimize transfer taxes is lifetime gifting. Transferring property to your heirs during your lifetime has certain advantages over waiting until you die. When you gift property that is expected to appreciate in value, you remove the future appreciation from your taxable estate.

There is one tradeoff to lifetime giving, though. Generally, if you gift property during your life, your basis in the property for federal income tax purposes carries over to the person who receives the gift. If you give your $1 million home that you purchased for $150,000 to your child, your $150,000 basis carries over to your child. If they sell the house without living in it for two years, capital gains tax may be due on the resulting gain.

But if you leave property to your heirs at death, they may get a "stepped-up" (or "stepped-down") basis in the property equal to the property's fair market value at the time of your death. If the home that you purchased for $150,000 is worth $1 million when you die, your heirs get the property with a basis of $1 million. If they then sell the home for $1 million, they pay no federal capital gains tax.

Federal Estate Tax

Are you worried about the national debt? (The answer is probably yes…)

The government is good at raising money, and the easiest people to get money from are rich people. The rich people who complain the least are dead rich people, so the government loves estate taxes.

As political parties toss the football back and forth, the estate tax laws are constantly changing, so it's important to work with an expert who can help you stay on top of any changes in the law.

For example, we're about to see a major change as the higher exemption sunsets on December 31, 2025. I like to joke that if you have a net worth of $20 million and you start feeling ill in the fall of 2025, you should die before the end of the year if you can time it. On New Year's Day of 2026, the exemption will likely be cut, meaning approximately 50% of an estate over about $6 million will be subject to estate taxes.

When property is transferred at death, it may be subject to estate tax. This is true whether or not the property goes through probate. For example, even though the funds in an IRA pass through a beneficiary designation, the funds are still potentially subject to estate tax. While Wisconsin doesn't currently have a state estate tax, Wisconsin residents may still have to pay federal estate taxes.

As with the gift tax, there are exceptions to the estate tax. For example, property that you leave to your spouse will generally not be subject to estate tax because there's a full deduction allowed for marital transfers. A similar deduction is available for property left to a charity.

As mentioned in the previous section, each individual has a $13.61 million exemption (in 2024) from gifts and estate tax combined. To be clear, this $13.61 million exemption covers both gifts and estates. Any portion of the exemption you use for gifts will not be available for your estate. This higher exemption of $13.61 million is set to sunset on December 31, 2025.

Promoting Good Behavior

Many people wonder, "If I leave money to my family members, how do I know they'll use it responsibly?"

There are lots of ways to give money. However, they really boil down to two ways:

1. Promote Good Behavior
2. Assume the Worst

If you want to promote good behavior among your heirs, there are several things you can do. You could match a family member's contributions to retirement savings, help them pay down debt, or add to an education fund.

My wife and I have decided to open Roth IRAs for each of our children this year for Christmas. It will be interesting to see if any of our kids read this book closely enough to find out what they are getting early.

You could also decide to gift money with no strings and assume the worst. If you give your son $1,000 in cash and your daughter-in-law shows up at Thanksgiving with a

$1,000 purse, you might turn red behind the ears, and the cranberry sauce might taste a bit off… But if you set your expectations low and assume that your family members are probably going to do stupid stuff with the money you give them, you may not be as disappointed if they do.

Income Taxes

The Tax Cuts and Jobs Act was signed into law by President Trump on December 22, 2017. This was the largest tax code overhaul in 31 years.

Here's a graph comparing tax brackets in 2017 (before the Tax Cuts and Jobs Act) and 2018 (after the Tax Cuts and Jobs Act) for someone with an income of $250,000 a year or less:

The tax brackets are set to return to what they were before the Tax Cuts and Jobs Act unless we have a Republican President and Congress and all the politicians get along. But let's face it—politicians getting along has never happened in the history of humanity. As a result, we can expect income taxes to change significantly over the next several years.

We have a progressive tax system, meaning that if you're in the 22% tax bracket, that doesn't mean all of your money is taxed at 22%. That just means the last dollar is taxed at 22%. Some of your income is taxed at 0%, some is taxed at 10%, some is taxed at 12%, and some is taxed at 22%.

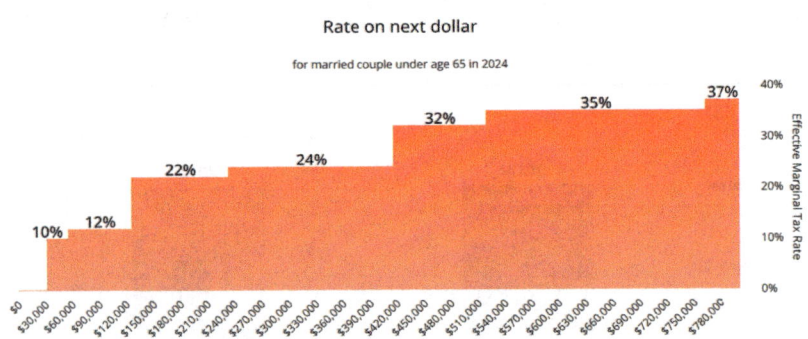

Provided by Joe Elsasser, Owner of Covisum

Capital gains have a different set of rates, and they're taxed differently. If you had only dividends and capital gains on your tax return, you would pay 0% until you have enough to fill the 12% ordinary income tax bracket. The 15% capital gains bracket extends from $94,051 - $583,750 of taxable income in 2024. Taxpayers with income at or above $583,751 are subject to the 20% capital gains.

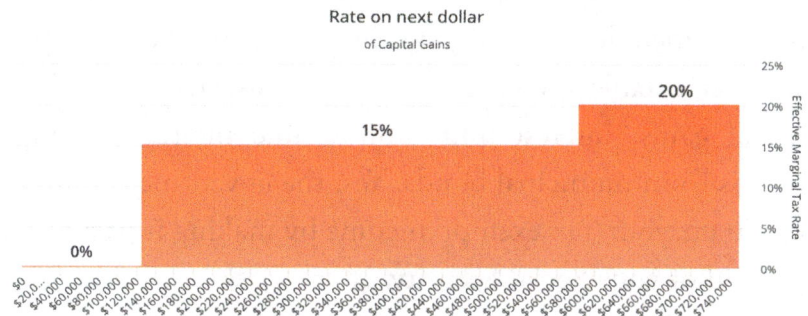

Provided by Joe Elsasser, Owner of Covisum

This is an important concept because it shows how capital gains taxation is actually linked to ordinary income. Once the combination of capital gains plus ordinary income pushes you above the threshold, your capital gains become taxable at 15%.

This structure really didn't change under the new tax bill, but because of a new larger standard deduction, the range at which it impacts you changes.

One of the best examples of unseen taxes is how retirement plans' required minimum distributions, taxed as ordinary income, can make Social Security taxable. If all you had on your tax return was Social Security, you would pay no federal income tax at all, but when you have other types of income, it can cause your Social Security to become taxable.

Let's walk through how that happens. Your "provisional income" includes 50% of your Social Security benefits, plus all other taxable income, including dividends and realized capital gains, interest, plus non-taxable interest earnings, such as from municipal bonds. Yes, the government found a way to tax your 'tax-exempt' income by making it part of the taxation of your Social Security.

This is what the tax system may actually look like:

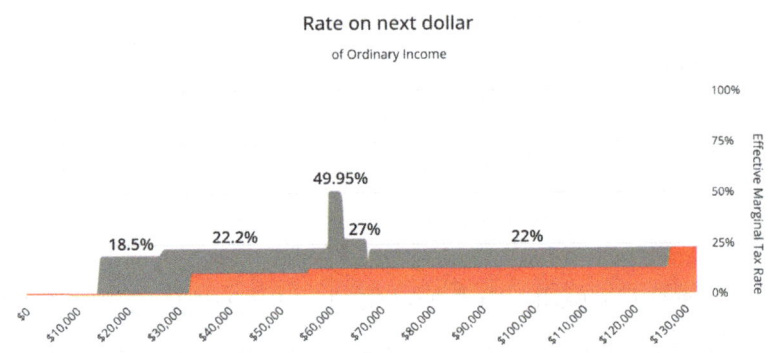

Provided by Joe Elsasser, Owner of Covisum

This is a special case for someone who has capital gains, Social Security, and other income combined, and some of that money may be taxed at almost 50%.

If you are saying, "Whoa – wait a minute, that spike occurred at the 12% bracket – how did that happen?", you are not alone.

Here's how it works: Imagine a couple in the 12% ordinary income bracket. You might expect that an additional $1,000 withdrawal would result in $120 in taxes.

But here's what actually happened. The $1000 withdrawal did get taxed at 12%, adding $120 to the tax bill. But then it caused $850 of Social Security Benefits to become taxable, adding another $102 to the tax bill, which then together caused $1,850 of Capital Gains that would have been taxed at 0% to become taxable, resulting in another $277.50 in Federal Income Tax. In short, on that $1,000, the couple lost 49.95% to federal income tax.

It's important to understand the tax bracket you're in and that it is possible to live at one income and pay taxes at another income.

This is done by controlling where you get your retirement income from. Having a forward-looking plan on where/what account you get your retirement income from is key to tax bracket management.

A Real Example

To understand how this works, let's look at a real example of a couple with an income of $52,420, putting them in the 12% bracket. Their income could increase by $40,000 to $92,800, without pushing them into a higher tax bracket.

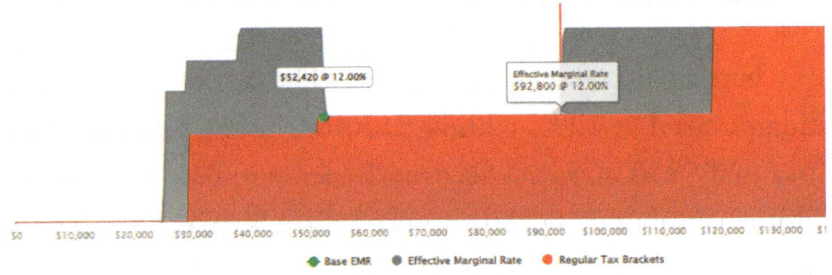

Provided by Joe Elsasser, Owner of Covisum

This is a perfect case to consider a Roth conversion of $40,000, especially if the couple has after-tax money to pay the tax on it (we don't want to take money out of a retirement account to pay the tax).

When it comes to Roth IRAs, there are only two times it makes sense to do a Roth conversion:

1) **Tax Bracket Arbitrage**: Taking advantage of being in a lower tax bracket now compared to what you expect in the future.

2) **After-Tax Dollars**: If you're retiring before age 65 and need after-tax dollars to get the tax credits associated with Affordable Care Act health insurance.

Why are these the only two instances?

If someone had $100,000 in an IRA, and they converted it to a Roth at the 25% tax bracket, they'd end up with $75,000. If that $75,000 doubles in size to $150,000, you have $150,000 tax-free. If they didn't do the conversion and the $100,000 got the exact same return and turned into $200,000, and they did a Roth conversion of the $200,000 at the 25% tax bracket, they still end up with $150,000. The person ends up with $150,000 either way. Unless there's a tax bracket arbitrage, it doesn't make sense to do a Roth conversion.

One of the biggest tragedies in America is the fact that a large number of people in the 12% tax bracket are saving money into their pre-tax retirement accounts, just to pay it back to the government at 18%, 22%, or even higher due to additional taxation of their Social Security benefits. If you explore tax strategies with an advisor, you can avoid this problem. For example, you could contribute to a Roth 401(k) or a Roth IRA. The best solution depends on your unique situation, so it's important to seek the advice of a professional before making a decision.

Tools for Tax Control

There are many ways to control taxes and plan to create tax-efficient retirements. Diversifying among different account types with different tax treatments, using tax-deferred products where appropriate, blending withdrawals from different account types instead of simply harvesting in sequential order, and paying close attention to which types of investments you hold in which account can all enhance the tax efficiency of your retirement income. **Properly blending withdrawals from different accounts lets you live in one tax bracket and pay taxes in a different tax bracket.**

Who's the best person to help you with your taxes? It's not the CPA or accountant. Remember —we consider tax preparers as historians for the IRS. Their job is to put numbers in boxes for what you did last year. Tax planning certainly involves looking at last year, but its main focus is reducing the numbers in the future.

If someone calls themselves a financial planner, but they haven't looked at your tax returns in two years, they're not a financial planner, they're an investment professional calling themselves a financial planner.

On December 20th 2019, a major piece of legislation known as the SECURE ACT was signed into law, and in 2022, the

SECURE Act 2.0 was passed. Tax laws are ever-changing, so it's important to stay up-to-date and understand that your tax strategies may have to adapt as the law changes.

Minimum distribution rules also change quite often. This year, the age was raised to 73.

A tool many of our clients over the age of 70 1/2 use is qualified charitable distributions (QCDs). This is a way of taking money out of a pre-tax position, such as an IRA and having it go straight to a charity, tax-free.

There's a huge difference between inheriting an IRA and an inherited IRA. A very large percentage of retirement accounts are cashed in at death by heirs. Instead of making it all taxable instantly, it may make sense to put it into an inherited IRA and spread that taxation out over up to ten years. It's especially important if it's a Roth IRA because then they could get ten more years of tax-free growth.

Family tax bracket management is critical. Understanding what tax bracket you're in compared to your heirs can make a difference on whether or not you should be pulling money out of retirement accounts, even if you don't need it, or if you should just be taking the minimums. In some cases, it may make sense to do a Roth IRA conversion. But you have to be careful that you don't make your Social Security benefits more taxable as a result. Every situation is different, so it's important to consult an expert when making these decisions.

If you pass away with a retirement account, there's a list of decisions that need to be made. I'm not showing you this list for you to learn it all, but rather to illustrate the complexities involved in estate planning and managing retirement accounts. Having a knowledgeable professional to navigate these complexities is often one of the most reassuring benefits of working with professional advisors.

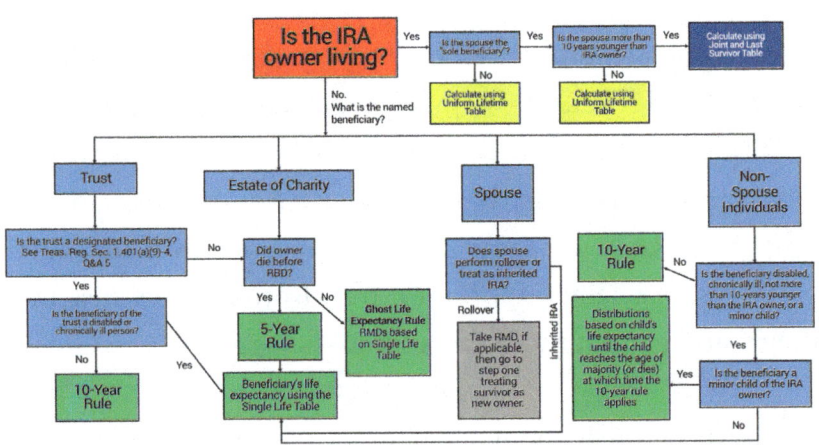

I'm only including this graphic so that you can see the complexities associated with retirement account planning. Note that these laws change often, and check with a professional advisor for current rules.

There are two ways of dealing with income taxes. You can either put your head in the sand, keep it simple, and overpay or you can work with an advisor to create a more complicated and personalized solution that saves you money.

CHAPTER 11

Long-Term Care and Nursing Homes

When I bring up planning for long-term care, a lot of people say, "Well, I'm just not going to a nursing home…"

The truth is, nobody in a nursing home wants to go there, but as much as 50% of the population may need to, so it's important to plan for that reality, even if you don't like it.

Some people believe they won't need to go to a nursing home because their well-intentioned children have promised to take care of them. Even if your children have promised to take care of you, it's important to prepare for a nursing home as a backup plan. If you end up having medical needs that go beyond the care your children can provide or need 24/7 supervision, you may need to go into a nursing home.

Also, no matter how well-intentioned your children are, it often happens that once children begin taking care of their elderly parents, they realize how big of a disruption to their lives it can be and wish Mom and Dad had prepared a backup option.

People go into a nursing home for one of two reasons: mental or physical. If it's physical, statistically, you're probably going to die or come home in three years or less. If it's mental, you may be living in a nursing home for twenty years or more. Three years and twenty years require vastly different planning.

In the United States, the average private room in a nursing home is $10,104 per month or $332 per day[1]. So, as you can see, planning for long-term care depends on each person's financial situation, and the importance of long-term care will only increase in the future as medical technology helps people live longer.

Understanding Medicaid

The government program that pays for long-term care is not Medicare; it's Medicaid.

Medicare will pay for up to 100 days of long-term care if you're coming from a hospital and rehabilitating, but our

---

[1] "Nursing Home Costs By State 2024," World Population Review, 2024.

concern is not 100 days—we need to figure out how to prepare for the possibility of years or even decades of care.

Medicaid is a needs-based program, meaning that a non-hospitalized spouse is allowed to have certain assets:

- A house ($750,000 of equity in 2024)
- $154,140 of investment assets
- One vehicle
- Clothing and other personal belongings
- Minimum Monthly Maintenance Needs Allowance
- The lessor of $3,853.50 or $3,114 + excess shelter allowance of $739.50 of monthly income
- Burial assets including vault & casket trust, burial trust, & plots
- $1,500 of life insurance
- $2,000 of cash

If you go above the limit in any one of these categories, Medicaid will not pay for your care.

The life insurance limit is very low, and life insurance agents tend not to explain that. If applying for Medicaid, many people end up having to cash in their life insurance when they're going into a nursing home.

Now, it's important to note that you're allowed to have these assets if you're married. But if you're not married, you're not allowed to have the house, the investment assets, or the vehicle.

There's currently a five-year lookback period for Medicaid qualification. On the application for Medicaid, they ask if you've gifted anything in the last 5 years. Your answer may affect your eligibility for Medicaid. As a general rule, we don't suggest you even apply for Medicaid unless you're sure that you will get it.

For example, let's say Joe develops Alzheimer's and needs to go into a Medicaid facility. Joe and his wife Mary live in a $300,000 house and have $400,000 in his retirement account. Mary could cash out the retirement account, pay taxes on the distribution, sell the $300,000 house, and buy a $600,000 house just so Joe can qualify for Medicaid and the couple can still protect their assets.

Another common piece of advice aimed at protecting home equity is to put your house in your children's names. Oftentimes, in the event of a nursing home stay, because of having assets higher than the above-listed Medicaid qualification numbers, the parents end up not qualifying for Medicaid anyway. Then the parent passes away, never qualified for Medicaid, and because they gifted the house to their children, the kids end up paying capital gains taxes at the sale of the home because it wasn't their personal residence. The result of following that advice was additional, unnecessary taxes for the kids. I cannot stress enough the importance of getting professional guidance before making such decisions.

Long-Term Care

There are three levels of assets to consider:

1. **Low Assets:** People with low enough assets that they'll qualify for Medicaid without a huge financial burden.

2. **High Assets:** People with high enough assets that they can afford to spend $120,000 a year on a nursing home. Typically, this means Social Security, maybe a pension, and at least a million and a half of liquid assets that they could draw an income from.

3. **In-Between:** Then, there's everybody in between. Everyone in this group needs to have some sort of plan, whether it's insurance or adjusting their finances to qualify for Medicaid. Where you fall in between the two brackets determines how we approach this. If you're closer to the top of the income bracket, you may just need a bare minimum insurance policy. If

you're closer to the bottom, you may need a more comprehensive long-term care insurance policy.

When we're looking at policies, we may seek out a five-year term due to the Medicaid lookback period. This approach limits your exposure to risk to five years, provided the non-hospitalized spouse is willing to adjust their lifestyle to qualify for Medicaid once the policy expires.

Planning for long-term care is definitely not a "cookie-cutter" situation. It requires an analysis of each family's unique needs. Also, planning for long-term care is more personal than many other financial decisions you'll make, and feelings can come into play.

For example, many people fail to adequately prepare for the cost of a nursing home stay because they find the idea unpleasant and hope their kids will take care of them.

Or some people go into the nursing home thinking, "I have assets, I should pay." Meanwhile, others feel that since they paid taxes their whole life, the government should pay for long-term care.

It's important to remove your feelings from the equation so you can make clear-headed decisions.

CHAPTER 12

Your Financial Team

Who Should Your Advisor Be?

Since a financial advisor is a long-term relationship, choosing the right one is critical to your financial journey.

Many advisors want to be the "quarterback" or CFO (Chief Financial Officer) of their clients' households.

However, I believe that you should be the "quarterback," CFO, or main decision-. You are the hero of the story—not the advisor.

In our firm, we act as the coach, not the quarterback. We never say "do this". Instead, we show you the pros and cons of each option and help you understand the impacts of your decision. Usually, we do this by showing you a good option, a better option, and in our opinion, the best option. Then it's up to you to choose. Our role is to educate you on your options and provide you with the guidance you need to make the right decisions for you and your family.

At the end of the day, it's your team and your life. You need to have confidence in making the decisions that fit your journey and situation.

We often say that our educated clients are our best clients. If you take the time to try to understand your financial decisions, you'll have greater success in making them. Our role as a coach is to help you become educated about the decisions you'll face.

Our role often extends beyond finances as we develop a long-term relationship. For example, we have assisted some of our retired clients with vacation planning, offering advice on destinations and tips for booking flights.

Working With a Fiduciary

When someone is licensed as a fiduciary, they are legally obligated to give their clients advice that is in their best interest.

For example, a car salesman receives a commission for selling a car. But if there were such a thing as a fiduciary car salesman, they would stay in contact with you so that as your family changed, they could make suggestions on different types of vehicles. They would only suggest cars that they knew would be a great fit for you and your family—instead of the most expensive cars that would give them the highest commissions.

A fiduciary is there for the long term and needs to understand the big picture of your finances. Meanwhile, a financial professional who is not a fiduciary may often be more motivated by making a sale in the short term than helping you in the long term.

If you have an advisor, think back on the conversations you've had with them. Do they ask questions about your situation or do they tell you they have the "perfect" product for you? If an advisor is more focused on a product than on you, they may not have your best interests at heart. What is the communication frequency from your advisor? How simple are the reports? Is it the same process each year?'

At our firm, to be as helpful and as fiduciary as possible, any commissions earned from selling an insurance product, 529 plans, 12b-1 fees, and/or trail revenue from variable annuities are donated to charity. We feel this is the best way to serve our clients as thoroughly as possible, as well as maintain our fiduciary/best interest for our clients' advice. We call this initiative Profits with Purpose and have established the

Hasenberg Financial Group Charitable Foundation, a fund of the Eau Claire Community Foundation.

A Practice Vs. A Business

Recently, in client meetings, I've been asked when I'm going to retire. I don't know if it's because I'm turning gray or because I mentioned I have grandkids...

Five or six years ago, I reached a point where I was financially able to retire. I decided not to retire because I love what I do and want to keep doing it. But that moment brought about a philosophical change in how I approached my career. I was no longer doing it for a paycheck–I was doing it because I love helping people. I realized that, by myself, I can only help a certain number of households, but if I hire other advisors and teach them everything I know, I can exponentially increase the number of households I'm able to help.

But everyone has to retire someday... When you're looking for an advisor, it's important to ask questions about who is on the team and what the future of the company will look like.

There's a difference between a practice and a business.

A friend of mine is a dentist. His office is made up of himself, a hygienist or two, and a receptionist. That's fine, as long as I don't get a toothache while he's on vacation.

Ten or fifteen years ago, I decided that I would transform my practice into a business, meaning that no part of the business is strictly dependent on me. I have taught every aspect of the business to somebody in the firm so that if a client needs help while I'm not available, they can get the help they need.

Our goal at Hasenberg Financial Group is a uniform client experience, meaning that no matter which rep you work with, you'll get the same advice for your situation. Each week, we share case studies and best practices so that our clients' experiences are consistent across advisors–and so that when I eventually retire, my clients won't have to miss a beat and can pick up right where they left off with one of the advisors who has trained with me for years.

When you're choosing an advisor, it's important to look beyond the specific advisor to the firm itself since this is a multi-decade relationship. Does the firm have a legacy plan in place? Will you be dependent on one advisor, or does the firm have other advisors who share your advisor's training and philosophy?

I want to have a multigenerational practice, meaning that we help families over generations, and that undertaking means my clients cannot be dependent on just me. Almost every meeting has more than one advisor in it so that if someone leaves, the client's experience can remain consistent. Our goal is to be a 100-year firm, so our focus is on creating a firm that can be sustained over decades.

What is your advisor's mindset? Are they focused on helping you or making money? Do you hear advisors bragging about "firing" misaligned clients because they have outgrown them? When you ask an advisor what they do, do they include a dollar amount in their response, such as, "We work with individuals who have $500k in assets..."? Advisors often say these things in sales pitches, hoping to attract bigger clients by making their firm seem like an exclusive club.

Because my firm's bottom line is about helping people, not making money, we've never set an account minimum to work with us, and we never fire clients to make room for wealthier clients. Our way of handling that situation is by adding advisors, not firing clients. We don't care how much money you have—we want to help you.

Your Financial Team

Your financial team is more than just your advisor. It is made up of your:

- Accountant
- Attorney
- Insurance P&C
- Life Insurance Professional
- Banker
- Investment Advisor

Your Financial Advisor: The Coach

Your financial advisor acts as the coach coordinating all of these players:

Accountants: There's a difference between planning and preparation. Your accountant's job is to put numbers in boxes for what you did last year. That's a hard enough job as it is, so your accountant doesn't have time to look into the future and determine how you can lower next year's tax bill. That's the job of a financial advisor. As your coach, we focus on tax planning: we've found that if we save you $1,000 in taxes, we become friends even quicker.

Attorney: How do you know if you have the right attorney? After you've worked with an attorney, ask yourself, "Would I go back or not?"

Insurance P&C: Do you have an umbrella policy? Since we don't sell insurance, we can let you know if we think you should have one or not. Many people don't know what an umbrella policy is, so we educate clients on it.

Life Insurance: Do you meet regularly with your life insurance agent? If you're not meeting at least once a year, it's a sign that you may not have the right life insurance professional.

Bankers: Do you have a contact at the bank, or is it a new face every time you go in? It's important to develop a relationship with a professional at the bank.

Investment Advisor: Remember, your investment advisor should not act as the quarterback and make decisions for you. On a scale from 1-10, one being the safest and ten being the riskiest, where do you think your investment portfolio is? If you think it's at a two and it's actually at a six, that's a problem. Do you know if your investment advisor is a fiduciary or not?

Long-Term Care Insurance Agent: Ideally, an agent who can evaluate your entire financial situation and make proper recommendations for policy type based on your situation. Bonus points if they donate all commissions to charity like we do.

If you need referrals to any of these team members, we have built a trusted network of professionals and would be happy to help you find the right fit.

Evaluating Your Financial Team

Do you pay your financial planner fees? Do you know how much the fees are? Is your financial planner a fiduciary? Lots of people have a financial planner, and they are aware that they are paying fees, but the question I want you to ponder is: Has the planner looked at your income tax returns in the last two years?

If they haven't, they may be more of an investment manager, not a financial advisor. Do not pay financial advisor-level fees to investment managers. If all you are looking for is investment management, there are lots of firms that can do that for considerably less fees than you are probably paying. The biggest fee that you'll probably pay is to Uncle Sam, which is why tax planning is such a crucial part of your plan.

The super-rich usually have what's called a family office, which is a private wealth management firm that provides the family with their own accountant, attorney, insurance agent, and so on. Why should this just be for the super-rich? At our firm, we provide a family office style of service. We do taxes in-house, and we have close relationships with other professionals that we can refer clients to.

If you build your financial team and have a relationship with each of these professionals, you can have the family office experience at any level of wealth.

CHAPTER 13

Hindsight is 20/20

After reading this book, you may feel like you have made some decisions you regret or missed out on opportunities in your financial planning.

Remember, we can't change the past. What matters is the present and how we move forward into the future.

When a boat is going across a lake, you can't change the wake going behind the boat. All you can do is change the direction that you steer the boat at this moment going forward. So if you've made mistakes in the past, that's okay. The good news is that you can take action today to start heading in a different direction.

Remember the wakes from Chapter 2? What do you want *your* family to say at your funeral? Do you want the end of the story to be, "we were left with such a mess" or "thank goodness everything was handled for us"?

Hopefully, you have some clear action items and have expanded your mindset. No matter what decisions you've made in the past, it's time to move toward the future.

Spending Money With Confidence

My job as a financial advisor is not to tell you to save all your money and pinch every penny you can. In fact, sometimes I have to convince my clients to spend money!

One of the greatest benefits of having a financial plan in place is understanding how much money you can comfortably spend. Often, people are tempted to be frugal because they fear they won't have enough money. But once we build a financial plan and understand how much you have, you'll be able to spend money with confidence.

On your last vacation, where did you sit on the plane? Many people opt for the cheapest tickets because they're afraid of spending too much money. But often, I tell my clients, "Go ahead and treat yourself to first-class tickets. Your plan shows that you have more than enough money to afford that."

When you sit down at a restaurant and look at the menu, do you look at the prices? Do you choose one of the cheaper items, even though you really want the steak? Knowing exactly how much you can spend gives you the freedom to choose based on what you want, not based on the price. Life is too short to miss out on amazing meals because you're afraid to spend money.

You've worked hard to earn money all of your life. Now, in retirement, it's time to enjoy the rewards of your hard work. A financial plan lets you know exactly how much you can comfortably spend, which gives you the confidence to spend your money on fantastic experiences.

My dad is one of those people who is unsure about spending money. About a decade ago, I created a retirement planning spreadsheet to show my dad that, with his spending habits, there was no scenario in which it would be possible for him to run out of money in retirement. I showed him and my mother that they had enough money to build a new one-floor home for retirement so they wouldn't have to worry about stairs as they aged.

They bought the house and looking back, my dad says it's one of the best decisions he's ever made. Yet if he didn't look at the numbers and see that there was no way for him to run out of money in retirement, he would likely have not bought the house for fear of running out of money.

Spending just two hours a year to review your goals, assess your progress, update your financial picture, and strategize tax minimization may be all it takes to build financial happiness.

If you're ready to achieve financial peace in just two hours a year, visit www.hasenberginc.com for more information.

ABOUT THE AUTHOR

Chris founded Hasenberg Financial Group in 1994 to help clients reach their personal financial goals through investment services, tax planning, retirement services, risk planning, and estate planning. His years of education, licensing, and experience make him especially adept at serving his clients in the most comprehensive way possible. He and his wife, Julie, have 7 children and step-children, two dogs, and they love being grandparents. When Chris is not in the office, he enjoys archery hunting (whitetails and turkeys), fishing, and staying active with golf, racquetball, and pickleball.

Made in the USA
Monee, IL
27 November 2024

70546767R00075